A STUDY OF THE PROBLEMS OF FILIPINO STUDENTS

IN THE UNITED STATES

A Thesis

University of Southern California

by

Aquilino B. Obando

1936

Reprinted in 1974 by

R AND E RESEARCH ASSOCIATES
4843 Mission Street, San Francisco   94112
18581 McFarland Avenue, Saratoga, California   95070

PUBLISHERS AND DISTRIBUTORS OF ETHNIC STUDIES
Editor: Adam S. Eterovich
Publisher: Robert D. Reed

LIBRARY OF CONGRESS CARD CATALOG NUMBER

74-76667

ISBN
0-88247-263-1

TABLE OF CONTENTS

LIST OF TABLES

This Book

Is Affectionately Dedicated

to the Memory

of My Father

Urbano Andres Obando

and My Mother

Tomasa Baloran Obando

CHAPTER I

THE PROBLEM

In 1898, the Spanish regime in the Philippine Islands came to an end. For the next thirty-seven years, the islands were under the yoke of the Government of the United States of America. During that time, there was a constant movement of Filipino students arriving in a continuous flow at the wide-open ports of the Union, where they came into contact with a democratic form of government, as well as educational opportunities for improvement.

Statement of the problem. The intention of this study was to make a general survey and investigation of conditions involving the problems which confront Filipino students, as well as to determine the nature of their life, in the colleges and universities of this Country. This will include the study of their aims, their native aptitudes, and their backgrounds.

The Filipino student in the United States is an agent of racial concord. This fact was established in the beginning of the close inter-relationship between the Government of the Philippine Islands and America, but it is only during the past twenty-five years that his great significance for international education has been truly recognized.

It would be difficult to exaggerate the vital meaning of student migrations to the cause of mutual understanding and friendship. Today, in the Philippines, American-trained nationals are dominant in the spread of Western ideas of education, public health, recreation, and social welfare. Similarly, Filipino students in the United States of America have interpreted to the American people the life and problems of their countrymen; with the utmost frankness they are pointing out the weaknesses and blunders of America's civilization and its impact on the rest of the world. If world unity and peace are ever to be realized, Americans may count on the Filipino student as an indispensable factor in the attainment of such a goal.

It has been a very great advantage to the Filipino students to be welcomed so warmly and enthusiastically into this Country, for it has enabled them to acquire knowledge and ability in the highly distinguished institutions of learning.

Justification of the problem. At the present time many thousands of them have completed their studies and have started forth to accomplish their burning desire, i.e., a successful career. These ambitious Filipino students in the United States of America will be men and women of tomorrow, who will in the near future be the leaders of their own country and people, and will carry on to the stepping-stone of their newly established form of Government.

Sources of materials. The writer endeavored to make a comprehensive survey of all the materials dealing with the problems of the Filipino students in the United States. The technique used was chiefly that of library research. Attempts have been made to obtain personal interviews with the students for further information about several of the problems involved in writing this thesis.

Related materials were secured in numerous bulletins and journals, a few books, annual reports, magazines, and newspapers. Some other sources have been used by the investigator. Attention was given particularly to bulletins, journals, and reports which are composed of the following: The Filipino Student Bulletin, with various volumes which are published by the Filipino Students' Christian Movement in America, edited by Manuel A. Adeva and several others. An article by Gertrude Hill Nystrum, in The Journal of Religious Education, gives some data regarding the percentage of the different types of students of the Country, and another article by W.W. Marquardt, in School and Society, which provided materials on the occupational outlook of the returned students to the Philippines as well as those who are still remaining on the mainland of the United States.

Also, articles have been read in the Institute of International

Education, by Ruth Crawford Mitchell, and from the War Department on official reports, dealing with the immigration law of the Filipino students in this Country.

Another material of special value to the writer in this respect is that of the Foreign Students in America, edited by Wheeler, King, and Davidson. This, as the title implies, does not deal specifically with Filipino students. Never-the-less, certain articles about them were discovered usable for the manuscript.

Organization of remainder of Thesis. The chapters of this study are composed of nine chapters, the first being the problem, with a discussion as to the statement of the problem, the justification of the problem, and the sources of materials. Chapter II covers the history of the Filipino student movement in this country. In the third chapter is found the financial resources of Filipino students; in the fourth, the geographical distribution of Filipino students in America. In Chapter V is developed the major educational interests of students; in the sixth, the cultural and social status of the Filipino students in the United States; in the seventh, the contribution of Filipino students; and in the eighth, is discussed the occupational outlook of Filipino students. The last chapter "Summary" gives the results of this investigation in order to set forth its use to others.

CHAPTER II

HISTORY OF THE FILIPINO STUDENT MOVEMENT

IN THE UNITED STATES

The presence of its students in this Country is of vital force in the development of progressive education for the inhabitants of the entire Philippine Archipelago. Therefore, the content of this chapter will be concerned with such problems as the following: the arrival of Filipino students in the United States of America; the Government pensionado students; the private students; the objective of the Philippine Government in sending students into this Country; the qualifications governing these students, in so far as the legislative act of 1924 is concerned; the number of students in the United States since the beginning of their movement to the present time.

Early legislative inducements for sending Filipino students to America. If the pages of history should be scanned, the tide of the present-day world-wide Filipino migration to the United States would be seen to have set in at a relatively early date. The life of Filipino students in this Country began at an earlier period than is perhaps generally realized. Though of prime origin, the movement of the Filipino students to the mainland of this Country seemed not to have gained rapidly.

The progress which the Filipino students have made in America inspires them and gives them the hope that they will go back home with the spirit of service to humanity. They will carry back with them the progressive essence with which they came into contact in this Country.

The timely influx of Filipino student pensionados[1] in the United States of America began in October, 1930. They were carefully selected by the Government of the Philippines as gifted and qualified students. Their ages ranged from sixteen to twenty years. The Government sent them to this Country for a period of four or more years of study and paid all their necessary expenses. The number of these students gradually increased from time to time, particularly during 1919, when the Philippines were badly in need of the idealistic and properly trained men and women with technical and scientific minds. Previous to this epoch, or as soon as the Philippine University was established, in 1908,[2] the Act was amended, so the only student pensionados sent by the Government from then on were those who had obtained degrees from that institution.

The movement of the Filipino students to this Country began as early as the American occupation of the Philippines. This included the private Filipino students, i.e., those who came of their own volition and with the aid of their wealthy parents, or who were wholly self-supporting. Their fine records as brilliant and conscientious students gained for them the respect and confidence of the American people. The excellence of their behavior served to combat adverse criticism and misrepresentation. The example set by these students was of twofold value; (1) It paved the way for a more complete understanding of the Filipino students who followed in their footsteps, and (2) it gave to the United States a group of young men and women from the Philippines who could really be termed missionaries.

The usefulness of the action of these students to the United States cannot be denied, in spite of the disorganized way in which it has been carried on. These students who have gone abroad now stand among the leaders of their nationals in America, and once safety and favorable conditions of usefulness are promised, many will return to their homeland. No doubt the destines of their Country and people will be in their hands, and there is every reason to believe that they will be equal to their opportunities.

The purposes of the Philippine Government in sending Filipino students to the United States of America are:[3] (1) to train young men and women to become ambassadors of goodwill and a lasting bond of friendship, as well as to promote better understanding of international relations; (2) to acquire an adequate comprehension and appraisal of the life and spirit of America; (3) to become successful and powerful leaders of tomorrow; (4) to study and familiarize themselves with American life at its highest and truest level; (5) and to know how to interpret the part of that life that the spirit and teachings of Christ have had in building up the institutions and the life of the Republic.

The Philippine Legislative Act of 1924. The Immigration Act of 1924, regarding the students coming from the Philippine Archipelago to the United States of America, is defined under Section 4 (e) as the following:

> An immigrant who is a bona fide student at least 15 years of age and who seeks to enter the United States solely for the purpose of study at an accredited school, college, academy, seminary, or university, particularly designated by him and approved by the Secretary of Labor, which shall have agreed to report to the Secretary of Labor, the termination of attendance of each immigrant student, and if any such institution of learning fails to make such reports promptly the approval shall be withdrawn. [4]

The enactment of the Philippine Legislative Act of 1924, Section 3 of Act Numbered Eight Hundred and fifty-four, entitled "An Act Providing for the Education of Filipino students in the United States of America and Appropriating for such Purpose the sum of Seventy-two thousand dollars in Money of the United States," is hereby amended as it states:

> After his selection and before his appointment each student shall be subjected to a physical examination by a physician designated by the Governor-General, and the appointment of such student shall depend on the favorable report of the physician so designated. Each student receiving an appointment shall be required to take the oath of allegiance to the Government of the United States, and to sign an agreement . . . to the effect that he will attend the educational institution designated by the Governor-General for the period of four years, or for such time as may be prescribed in his appointment, . . . that he will conform to all regulations, rules, and laws of said institution and such other regulations as may be prescribed by the Department of Public Instruction . . . Provided, that upon the termination of his studies in the United States, in conformity with this

Act and the terms of his appointment and agreement, he will return to the Philippine Islands, and within two months after his return will take a civil-service examination, competitive or non-competitive, . . . Provided, that should the interests of the service so warrant, the Director of Civil Service, may, with the approval of the Secretary of Public Instruction in lieu of giving special examination, extend the period within which returning student shall take a civil-service examination until the dates for the next regular examination.[5]

Number of Filipino students in the United States. In general, there is no accurate figure which has ever been given concerning the number of Filipino students in the United States of America. Different surveys and statistics which have been found by the writer, and which will be shown in various tables of this chapter, have unequal conclusions. Although, questionnaires have been distributed among the many leading colleges and universities in the United States, several of the smaller institutions were not being represented at all. Thus the students in those particular schools were not included in the survey.

Reference to surveys on the Annual Report of the Institute of International Education[6] and that of the Directory of Filipino Students in America[7] for the academic year of 1934-1935, will give a complete verification of the statements made above. The former established the fact that the total number of students was four hundred and seventeen, while that of the latter gave a total of five hundred-forty-eight, with a difference of one hundred and thirty-one students. These were the results obtained by each survey in that same identical academic year. The sum total of students reported by the investigator is the only figure known to the public at large.

The number of Filipino Government students in the United States, was recorded by the Friendly Relations Committees of Foreign Students,[8] is shown on Table I. The first Government students sent to this country in 1903 were one hundred and three; in 1904, forty-three; in 1905, thirty-nine; in 1906 to 1912, eight students for each year, a total of fifty-six; in 1919, one hundred and thirty; in 1920, forty-six, in 1921 only three students; in 1922, thirteen, in 1923, thirty-four; and in 1924, thirty-seven students. The wholly self-supporting students have not been recorded for these periods of time.

Table I

Number of Filipino Pensionado Students in the
Colleges and Universities of the
United States, 1903-1924*

Academic Year	Number of Students
1903	103
1904	43
1905	39
1906-12	56
1919	130
1920	46
1921	3
1922	13
1923	34
1924	37

*W. Reginald Wheeler, Henry H. King, and Alexander B. Davidson, ed., The Foreign Student in America, Commission on Survey of Foreign Students in the United States of America (New York: Association Press, 1925).

In Table II there is shown the number of all the types of students, the pensionados and the private students, in the academic years from 1921 to 1935. According to the statistics which have been found in the Fourteenth Annual Report of the Director of the Institute of International Education,[9] the number of students indicates that in the academic year of 1921 to 1922 there were five hundred ninety-four students; in 1922-1923, six hundred forty-nine; in 1923 to 1924, five hundred ninety-one; in 1924 to 1925, six hundred; in 1925 to 1926, five hundred seventy-one; in 1926 to 1927, seven hundred forty-five, in 1928 to 1929, one thousand seventy-three; in 1929 to 1930, eight hundred ninety-six; in 1930 to 1931, eight hundred ninety; in 1931 to 1932, six hundred forty-two; in 1932 to 1933, five hundred twenty-one; in 1933 to 1934,[10] four hundred eighty-nine; and in 1934 to 1935,[11] five hundred forty-eight.

Table II

Number of All Types of Filipino Students in
the Colleges and Universities of the
United States, 1921*-1935*

Academic Year	Number of Students
1921-1922	594
1922-1923	649
1923-1924	591
1924-1925	600
1925-1926	571
1926-1927	754
1928-1929	1073
1929-1930	896
1930-1931	890
1931-1932	642
1932-1933	521
1933-1934	489
1934-1935	548

*Institute of International Education. Fourteenth Annual Report of the Director (New York: Bulletin No. 4, October 1, 1933).

*Manuel A. Adeva, ed., Directory of Filipino Students in the United States (New York: 1934-1935).

This same table also indicates the irregularity of attendance which is due mainly to those students who are wholly self-supporting while going to school. When these students are not able to secure good jobs before the opening of the semester, they are apt not to be able to secure good jobs and go back to college until the next academic year. Many of them stop for a year or so, to get money enough for their expenses for the succeeding school year. On the other hand, the influence of the economic depression which occurred during the past four years, 1930 to 1934, was evident in the reduction of Filipino students enrollment in the colleges and universities in the United States. It is very interesting to note, that such enrollment of students gradually decreased during that period of time.

FOOTNOTES

[1]W. Reginald Wheeler, Henry H. King, and Alexander B. Davidson, ed., The Foreign Student in America, Commission on Survey of Foreign Students in the United States of America, (Association Press, New York: 1925), p. 17.

[2]Encarnation Alzona, History of Education in the Philippines (Manila: University of the Philippines Press, 1925), p. 273.

[3]Wheeler, King, Davidson, op. cit., p. 13.

[4]Ruth Crawford Mitchell, "Foreign Students and Immigration Laws of the United States," Institute of International Education (New York: Bulletin No. 1, Eleventh Series, January 1, 1930), p. 8.

[5]War Department, U.S.A. Annual Reports, 1907. Acts of the Philippine Commission Public Resolution (Washington: Government Printing Office, September 16, 1906--October 31, 1907), 10:470.

[6]Institute of International Education, The Institute of International Education, Sixteenth Series, Sixteenth Annual Report of the Director (Bulletin No. 1, New York: October 1, 1935), p. 41.

[7]Manuel A. Adeva, ed., Directory of Filipino Students in the United States (New York: 1934-1935), p. 31.

[8]Wheeler, King, Davidson, op. cit., p. 17.

[9]Institute of International Education, The Institute of International Education, Fourteenth Series, Fourteenth Annual Report of the Director (Bulletin No. 4, New York: October 1, 1933), p. 63.

[10]News Bulletin, The Institute of International Education, New York: February, 1934, 9:10.

[11]Adeva, loc. cit.

CHAPTER III

FINANCIAL RESOURCES OF FILIPINO STUDENTS

One among the most immediate and often the most insistent problems of the Filipino students in the United States is that of employment. The fierce struggle to make a living while attending school is the chief concern of the majority of the students; especially is this true of the self-and-partially-supporting ones. In this chapter probably everyone is interested in knowing how many of them are prospering financially, how many are barely holding their own, and how many are unfortunately slipping behind in the struggle, and why.

First of all, one wants to know the range and character of their jobs, and their reactions to existing circumstances. Further, one wishes to determine their financial status, their means of support, and their living conditions while in American colleges and universities.

The Filipinos may be classified according to sources of their financial means, such as those who are supported fully by the Philippine Government and institutions, those who are wholly self-supporting while going to college, and those who are partly supported by their parents, friends, or relatives.

The pensionado students. The term "pensionados" refers to those students who are supported by the Philippine Government and institutions, or by parents, or relatives, or friends.[1] But the Government students are mostly concerned in this matter. The Government support of the full pensionado students includes an allowance of seventy dollars per month (eighty dollars if the student is a resident of New York City) for subsistence, quarters, laundry, and other expenses, together with payment of necessary college expenses, including tuition fees, books, medical attention, and clothing. The students who were sent by the Philippine Government in later years to the mainland of the United States of America were men and women who had been in the employ of the Government for a number of years, but they were chosen for their exceptional interests and abilities in certain special fields of study. Every one of these students contracts to serve the Government one and one-half years for each year of his scholarship, at the regular rate of compensation for such service. This system has worked out very well and it is surprising to note how many important places in the Philippine Government are held by former students pensioned by the Government. These scholars were graduates of the University of the Philippines. The first pensionados who were delegated to this country were undergraduates, because the State University, the University of the Philippines, had not yet been founded. These students took a longer period of time to finish their courses of study than those students who came later. The Government spent more money for them than the amount expended on the present-day students.

The percentage of this group of students as stated by Nystrum is only five.[2] The report on the Friendly Relations Committees Among Foreign Students[3] shows 9.8 per cent.

Self-supporting students. The entirely self-supporting students are those who earn money for all of their needs while on their way through college.[4] This includes board, room, tuition fees, books, laundry, clothing, and other miscellaneous expenses, but it is believed that most of these students are doing their own washing, ironing, and cooking. This type of student is mostly faced with the problems mentioned.

Some students who otherwise could go to college for full time during the regular sessions have to work full time during vacations, summer time, and week-ends to earn enough money to meet the major part of their expenses. Many work on fruit ranches, where they are able to earn from one hundred and eighty dollars to two hundred dollars during the season of three months. In many instances students who have had more experience in fruit picking are able to earn more by doing piece work rather than going in as a day laborer. In this way, they are able to receive from two to two and a half dollars a day, and although the work is not steady, it gives them plenty of time for outdoor sports and other recreations. Many are employed in summer resorts and camps, where they are paid from thirty-five to forty-dollars a month, with board and lodging. Others work in hotels as waiters and bell boys. Still others work in apartment houses. Several of the students are also going for the whole summer to the canneries in Alaska, where they may save from one hundred and fifty to two hundred dollars.

A large number of the fully self-supporting are part-time students. Some are employed in various capacities, such as clerks in post offices and in restaurants, either as helpers in the kitchen or as waiters. Most of the students having post office jobs are able to make arrangements to go on the night shift and are thus able to attend classes during the day. Those who cannot take advantage of this plan may avail themselves of the opportunity of the night division courses, without any appreciable difference from the day classes.

With regard to the self-help students who work besides going to school, Dean says the following:

> A boy who works outside of school is learning how to earn money, learning how to meet people, learning how to adapt himself to life situations, and learning the applications of knowledge to real life.
> All honor to boys and girls who work outside of school, whether they work because of economic necessity, for spending money, or for the sheer delight of work.[5]

The self-supporting students are found everywhere in the Union; the success of an individual depends largely upon his ability to adapt himself to the new environment and his willingness to do any sort of work.

Compelled to work at most menial tasks outside of school and frequently to give up school for a quarter semester, or a year, still they toil on, and many of them have obtained their Ph.D. degree and other distinctions in Medical, Dentistry, Law, Philosophy, or other courses.[6]

This type leads by a great majority over the other groups. Being a student and a worker keeps a student very busy, but he will probably make better grades than the boy who does not have to work at all. Earl J. Miller, Dean of Men at the University of California at Los Angeles, says:

> Figures show that those working their way through make grades that are a trifle better than those who are not required to work. Of course, we have no way of knowing grades these working students might make if they were unburdened. They might be even better. But I do not say that working does not seriously interfere with studies.[7]

Never-the-less, they may well be proud of themselves, and they will be congratulated and praised as soon as they accomplish their high ambitions.

The availability of work often determines the student's choice of a profession. Because they have to work in order to go to school, some of the students select only those courses that will give them more time to study and that can be taken without jeopardizing their work. It is obvious, therefore, that many of the Filipino students in this group are taking courses for which they do not have special inclination or aptitude.

Referring to Nystrum, in so far as the percentage of these scholars is concerned, she states that there are 63 per cent who are wholly dependent upon themselves for financial support.[8] The examination of five hundred seventy-five information cards filled out by Filipino students at the office of the Friendly Relations Committee Among Foreign Students, picked at random, reveals the fact that 87.3 per cent are entirely self-supporting.[9] Students of this class enroll in colleges and universities located in places where they can surely secure sufficient work. This is in order that they may not lose the opportunity for steady employment which will make it possible for them to complete their college course and so obtain a college degree.

One of the reasons for the Filipino movement to the United States has been the opportunities for self-support in the American institutions of learning. This undoubtedly accounts for the high percentage of the students who are wholly dependent upon their own efforts for a livelihood. The respect which a self-supporting student commands, and the willingness on the part of many Americans to help those who are working their way through college, has greatly encouraged many a newly-arrived Filipino student in this country. Colleges and universities in certain sections of the United States offer more opportunities for self-support than others, because of the climatic conditions.

These students are beset with more difficulties at the present time than heretofore. However, there is much consolation for them, for everything else being equal, a self-help student will reach his goal barring economic handicaps. He may be delayed, but eventually he will be there.

A revelation made by Higinio Mendoza states the following:

He went to America in August, 1919, arriving there with only three dollars and fifty cents to his name for he is of (came from) a poor family. How to get a medical education was his chief problem. Naturally, the only course to follow is via the classical "Self-supporting". It took him up to (until) 1928 to reach his goal, fighting barehandedly, but (he) got there. This was made possible because he had fixed his goal.

After his course had been attained, he had obtained hospital jobs in a city in the United States for two years. These positions offered enough money and comforts to have induced him to hang onto them. But there was another goal (for which) that he aimed: to return home and be amongst his people. This brought him home in October, 1930.[10]

The partially self-supporting students. The partially self-supporting ones[11] are the recipients of financial aid from their parents, relatives, or friends. The amount received is usually enough to cover the student's tuition fees, books, and clothing, leaving him to work for his room and board, which he usually does by waiting on tables. Others take a job as school boy and help about the house from three to four hours in a day in exchange for room and board and a few dollars per week. The work generally involves house cleaning, cooking two meals (frequently breakfast and dinner), and dish washing.

Students most successful in this kind of work are those who have patience and fortitude.

This type of student shows the least percentage, as will be seen on Table III. This table shows that there were only 2.9 per cent in 1925, that 25 per cent earn about 75 per cent of their expenses, and 12 per cent earned 50 per cent or less in 1935. The sons of the wealthy people have the greatest opportunity to continue their studies for this reason. On the other hand, there are only a very few of those who have friends, brothers, or relatives willing to give them financial aid for their college work.

Table III

Percentage of Filipino Students in the Colleges
and Universities of the United States,
1925* and 1935*

Types of Students	Percentage	
	1925	1935
Philippine Government pensionados	9.8	
Wholly self-supporting students	87.3	63.0
Partially self-supporting students	2.9	
Earn 75% of expenses		25.0
Earn 50% of expenses		12.0

*Gertrude Hill Nystrum, "America as Filipinos See It," Religious Education, The Journal of Religious Educational Association, 28: January, 1933-October, 1935.

*W. Reginald Wheeler, Henry H. King, and Alexander B. Davidson, ed., The Foreign Student in America, Commission on Survey of Foreign Students in the United States of America (New York: Association Press, 1925).

FOOTNOTES

[1] Prof. I. Panlasigui, "The Filipinos in the United States," The Filipino Students Bulletin, 6:3, May, 1927.

[2] Gertrude Hill Nystrum, "America as Filipinos See It," Religious Education, The Journal of Religious Educational Association, 28:151, January, 1933-October, 1935.

[3] Wheeler, King, Davidson, op. cit., p. 159.

[4] Ibid.

[5] Arthur Dean, "Working Outside School Hours," Journal of Education, 112:481, July-December, 1930.

[6] Manuel A. Adeva, ed., The Filipino Student Bulletin, 8:2, March 1931.

[7] Ralph W. Trueblood, ed., The Los Angeles Times, Part 1, October 20, 1935.

[8] Nystrum, loc. cit.

[9] Wheeler, King, Davidson, loc. cit.

[10] Higino Mendoza, "To the Filipino Students in the United States," The Filipino Bulletin, 13:5, December, 1934.

[11] Wheeler, King, Davidson, loc. cit.

CHAPTER IV

GEOGRAPHICAL DISTRIBUTION OF FILIPINO

STUDENTS IN AMERICA

An unorganized group of Filipino students, after devious migration, have finally settled in many sections of the United States. This is particularly true on the Pacific Coast, which is the so-called Western section of the Country. This constitutes the raw material of this study. The range of the investigation includes primarily those students in the Eastern section and those in the Middle-western section, in addition to the one that has just been mentioned. The scope of the study embraces the occupational, economic, and climatic conditions which determine the choice of the students in their selection of places to live.

The distribution of the students in American institutions is uneven; in some sections there are more than seems advisable, while in other parts of the Country there are none at all. As yet, there has been no scheme devised by which these students can be divided equally among the different colleges and universities of the Country.

The eastern section. The colleges and universities in the Eastern section of the United States have a smaller Filipino student population than the Middle-western and the Western institutions.[1] The self-supporting students are quite few in number because of the fact that the climate is too cold during the winter and too hot during summer times, and jobs are too poorly paid for this type of students. Consequently, they established themselves in the other sections of the Country. The Filipino student pensionados are mostly found in the institutions of learning in the Eastern part of the United States. They attend particularly the leading colleges and universities, such as Cornell,

Columbia, Harvard, Indiana, Chicago, Yale, Massachusetts, Institute of Technology, and others.

The students who are entirely dependent upon their own resources are found in the cities of New York, Philadelphia, Washington, D.C. and other big cities, where there seem to be ample opportunities to secure jobs. Later afternoon and evening classes are mostly attended by the majority of these students.

Table IV shows that in 1930, there were nine states and a district which constitute the Eastern section of the Country where the Filipino students were found.[2] Among these were Connecticut, Louisiana, Maryland, Massachusetts, New Jersey, New York, North Carolina, Pennsylvania, and West Virginia. The colleges and universities of the States of New York, the District of Columbia, Massachusetts, Louisiana, and Pennsylvania had the greatest enrollments. There were ten colleges and universities in the State of New York where Filipino students are obtaining their education.

In 1930, there were more students found in that part of the Country than in 1935, i.e., there were one hundred and thirty-nine students, including sixteen women and one hundred and twenty-one men, in 1930, while there were only seventy-three students, three of which were women and seventy men, in 1935.

In the academic year of 1934-1935, there were eight states including one district in that section of the Union where Filipino students were enrolled.[3] These were Alabama, Connecticut, the District of Columbia, Louisiana, Maryland, Massachusetts, New York, Pennsylvania, and West Virginia. The colleges and universities of the States of New York and the District of Columbia had the largest numbers of students.

The Mid-western section. In the Mid-western section of the United States there is an unusually large group of self-supporting students.[4] This is especially true in the following cities: Chicago, Illinois; Lawrence, Kansas;

Table IV

Filipino Students in the Eastern Colleges and Universities of the United States, 1929-1930* and 1934-1935*

States	Women		Men		Total	
	1930	1935	1930	1935	1930	1935
Alabama				1		1
Connecticut			1	1	1	1
Dist. of Columbia			36	21	36	21
Louisiana	1		15	4	16	4
Maryland			2	6	2	6
Massachusetts	2	1	14	4	16	5
New Jersey			3		3	
New York	12	2	38	25	50	27
North Carolina			1		1	
Pennsylvania	1		11	5	12	5
West Virginia			2	3	2	3
Grand Total	16	3	123	70	139	73

*Bruno Lasker, Filipino Immigration (Chicago: The University of Chicago Press, 1931).

*Manuel A. Adeva, ed., Directory of Filipino Students in the United States (New York City: 1934-1935.

Iowa City, Iowa; and Ann Arbor, Michigan. The students found there because available employment could be had in post offices, factories, hotels, restaurants, club houses, and many other places which supply work to them. Most of the scholars in Chicago attended classes at Lewis Institute. In Detroit, the students were going to technical schools where they could be employed on a full-time basis during the day, giving them practical training at the various factories.

According to Table V, the State of Illinois leads with the greatest number of students; in 1930 there were thirty-nine, the rest of the states ranged from thirty down to one student registered.

Table V

Filipino Students in the Middle-Western Colleges
and Universities of the United States,
1929-1930* and 1934-1935*

States	Women		Men		Total	
	1930	1935	1930	1935	1930	1935
Illinois	3		137	39	140	39
Indiana			17	17	17	17
Iowa			22	6	22	6
Kansas			30	14	30	14
Kentucky			4	1	4	1
Michigan	2	3	27	20	29	23
Missouri			11	6	11	6
North Dakota				1		1
Ohio			11	3	11	3
Oklahoma			3	4	3	4
South Dakota			3	1	3	1
Wisconsin			7	6	7	6
Grand Total	5	3	272	118	277	121

*Bruno Lasker, Filipino Immigration (Chicago: The University of Chicago Press, 1931).

*Manuel A. Adeva, ed., Directory of Filipino Students in the United States (New York City: 1934-1935).

In regard to the data shown on Table V, in 1930 there were two hundred seventy-seven students.[5] Five women and two hundred seventy-two men comprised this total. During the year of 1935, a total of one hundred twenty-one students were enrolled in the mid-western institutions of the Country; this number included three women and one hundred eighteen men.[8]

The Western section. The statistics disclosed in this chapter, which were compiled by the writer of various surveys and investigations, prove that the western section has the largest population of Filipino students on the campuses of similar colleges and universities among the three geographical divisions of the United States.[7] As previously mentioned, it is a fact that more than eighty-seven per cent of these students in America are wholly dependent upon their own efforts for support. Because of the high percentage of this type, they have enrolled in colleges and universities located in places where they can surely find work.

The influence of a brother, or a relative, or a friend is also a factor for this distribution of students. A student goes to a particular university not primarily because he believes that such institution can give him the best training in his field of study, but because he happens to have a brother, a relative or an intimate friend in that part of the Country. He will always expect his friend or relative to be able to assist him.

Favorable climatic conditions is still another reason why the Western colleges and universities have the greatest enrollment.

The weather being mild and equable makes clothes less expensive in the middle-western section. In the East it is necessary to have a varied outfit, one for the spring, and much warmer one for the winter. In summer it is necessary to have very cool garments. The Filipino students feel, as do the American people and others, that the climate in the West is the most healthful in the United States. This is a saving to them in their budget for dress and other expenses. The money saved will be used for their studies and other miscellaneous charges. They feel it is more economical to live on the Pacific Coast than anywhere else. The commodity prices are very much lower here than in any other section of the country.

In Washington State, there is a great number of the Filipino students because they are attracted by a low tuition fee. For this reason, together with the availability of work for room and board, they gather there in great numbers.

A large number of the self-supporting students in San Francisco and other large cities on the Pacific Coast are employed in various capacities. During the summer months this section of the Country offers students sufficient employment for them to earn enough money for their college expenses. In the State of California, as is shown in Table VI, a great number of students is over-crowding the many leading institutions of learning, because of the many chances to work on fruit ranches and summer resorts during vacations. It is the most crowded of all the States of this section, especially in the cities of San Francisco, and Los Angeles. Some of the students work in the canneries in Alaska after school days.

During the academic year of 1929-1930, there were fourteen states where Filipino students were enrolled;[8] in 1934-1935, there were twelve states.[9] This revealed that there is a great difference of enrollment between now and then.

Every institution in the United States is known for its outstanding leaders in special departments. Johns Hopkins University is known for its excellent school of medicine, Columbia University for its pre-eminent school of education, and the University of Southern California is known for its schools of sociology and international relations. And still another outstanding institution of its kind in this country is that of the California Institute of Technology, which is widely known for its school of science. Several of the Filipino students have attended these fine schools with the exception of the latter, taking their advanced degrees.

Table VII indicates that in the academic year of 1929-1930, in the Eastern Colleges there were one hundred thirty-nine students; in the Middle-western, there were two hundred seventy-seven; and in the Western colleges, there were four hundred eighty.[10] That of 1934-1935 shows seventy-three in the Eastern colleges; one hundred twenty-one in the Middle-western; and three hundred fifty-four in the Western colleges and universities.[11]

Table VI

Filipino Students in the Western Colleges and
Universities of the United States,
1929-1930* and 1934-1935*

States	Women		Men		Total	
	1930	1935	1930	1935	1930	1935
Arizona			10	4	10	4
California	4	1	159	195	163	196
Colorado			4	9	4	9
Idaho			12	4	12	4
Minnesota	2		25	13	27	13
Montana			6	6	6	6
Nebraska			28	5	28	5
Nevada			2	1	2	1
New Mexico			1	1	1	1
Oregon			73	15	73	15
Texas			1		1	
Utah			12		12	
Washington	3		137	99	140	99
Wyoming			1	1	1	1
Grand Total	9	1	471	353	480	354

*Bruno Lasker, Filipino Immigration (Chicago: The University of Chicago Press, 1931).

*Manuel A. Adeva, ed., Directory of Filipino Students in the United States (New York City: 1934-1935).

Again, according to Nystrum, the geographical distribution of the Filipino students in the United States shows ten per cent are attending the Eastern colleges and universities; thirty-four per cent are found in the Middle-western institutions; and fifty-six per cent are in the Western colleges and universities of higher learning. [12]

With regard to the tables shown above, the distribution of Filipino

Table VII

Students in the Colleges and Universities Enrolled in Every Section of the United States, 1929-1930* and 1934-1935*

Sections	Women		Men		Total	
	1930	1935	1930	1935	1930	1935
Eastern	16	3	123	70	139	73
Middle-Western	5	3	272	118	277	121
Western	9	1	471	353	480	354
Grand Total	30	7	866	541	896	548

*Bruno Lasker, Filipino Immigration (Chicago: The University of Chicago Press, 1931).

*Manuel A. Adeva, ed., Directory of Filipino Students in the United States (New York City: 1934-1935).

students in 1929-1930 shows that there were thirty-six states out of the forty-eight where they were found. In 1934-1935 only thirty-three states showed any Filipino students.

A survey of the three sections during the academic year of 1929-1930, disclosed the fact that there were thirty women and eight hundred sixty-six men students, a total of eight hundred ninety-six. In the academic year of 1934-1935, there were only seven women and five hundred forty-one men students, a total of five hundred forty-eight.

FOOTNOTES

[1]Wheeler, King, Davidson, op. cit., p. 161.

[2]Bruno Lasker, _Filipino Immigration_ (Chicago: The Universities of Chicago Press, 1931), p. 437.

[3]Adeva, loc. cit.

[4]Wheeler, King, Davidson, op. cit., p. 160.

[5]Lasker, loc. cit.

[6]Adeva, loc. cit.

[7]Wheeler, King, Davidson, loc cit.

[8]Lasker, loc. cit.

[9]Adeva, loc. cit.

[10]Lasker, loc. cit.

[11]Adeva, loc. cit.

[12]Nystrum, loc. cit.

CHAPTER V

MAJOR EDUCATIONAL INTERESTS OF FILIPINO STUDENTS

The Filipino students in the United States have varied tasks to accomplish and to perform. Some of them came here to learn arts and trades, several are employed in industrial plants and factories, others are enrolled in various colleges and universities in the Union, and still others are devoting their time to specialization along certain lines which may prove helpful and profitable to Filipino culture.

It would be of great interest, therefore, to note in this chapter the different schools attended, or the fields of study a student may be interested in. In this respect, the different schools and colleges having the largest group and those having the smallest will be shown. This problem involves the discussion of such topics as their major fields of interest, their favorite subjects, the growth of curriculum, and the participation of women students.

Schools and Colleges attended by students. The variety of professions selected by the Filipino students in the colleges and universities of the United States is quite interesting and encouraging, for it indicates in some degree the spirit and attitude of these youths toward the improvement of their Country.

Reports on the various courses of study in which Filipino students are enrolled are shown in Table VIII. These basic courses of study were compiled from Lasker's Filipino Immigration,[1] and from The Directory of Filipino Students in the United States,[2] respectively. The students have indicated their major educational interests, which cover forty-five fields of endeavor in the former and fifty-four in the latter, ranging from agriculture to zoology. Most of the students show rich promise of successful careers in

Table VIII

Courses of Study Elected by Filipino Students in the American Colleges and Universities 1929-1930* and 1934-1935*

Major Subjects	Number of Students	
	1930	1935
Agriculture	51	12
Agriculture Engineering		1
Agronomy		2
Anthropology		1
Architecture	4	4
Arts and Science		11
Biology	5	1
Botany	3	1
Business		3
Business Administration	31	10
Chemistry	6	8
Chemical Engineering		2
Civil Engineering	10	
Commerce	55	23
Dentistry	2	1
Economics	6	9
Education	94	56
Electrical Engineering	10	5
Engineering	59	32
English	20	5
Entomology		1
Fine Arts		6
Finance		3
Foreign Service	2	
Fishery		1
Forestry	3	1
History	3	6
Horticulture		2
Household Economics	6	
Journalism	5	7
Languages		2
Latin	1	
Law	1	12
Letters, Arts and Sciences	99	31

(Continued)

Table VIII (Cont.)

Major Subjects	Number of Students	
	1930	1935
Liberal Arts	113	28
Library Science	1	
Literature		1
Mathematics	5	4
Mechanical Engineering	19	70
Medicine	15	4
Military Science		5
Mining Engineering	10	20
Music	4	4
Natural Science		1
Naval Architecture	2	
Nautical		1
Nursing	1	
Osteopathy		1
Pharmacy	4	5
Philosophy	4	4
Physiology	1	
Political Science	11	12
Pre-medical	15	
Psychology	1	2
Public Health	1	
Railway Engineering	1	
Real Estate		1
Religious Education		1
Science	10	1
Social Science	12	4
Sociology		5
Theology	19	14
Unclassified	147	152
Veterinary Medicine	5	2
Zoology	4	2

*Bruno Lasker, Filipino Immigration (Chicago: The University of Chicago Press, 1931).

*Manuel A. Adeva, ed., Directory of Filipino Students in the United States (New York City: 1934-1935).

their chosen professions and fields of interests. Many of them show marked ability and great enthusiasm--qualities that will greatly aid them.

Courses of study chosen by Filipinos. The most popular courses among the Filipino students in the academic year of 1929-1930 indicates that liberal arts ranked first, with one hundred thirteen enrolled; letter and sciences and engineering which includes civil, mechanical, electrical, and railway engineering followed, with ninety-nine enrolled in each field; education ranked the third, with ninety-four students registered; commerce ranked fourth, with fifty-five students; agriculture ranked fifth, with fifty-one students; and the rest of these courses ranged from thirty-one to one students. Furthermore, there were one hundred forty-seven students reported unclassified.

The academic year of 1934-1935 shows that engineering, which includes agricultural engineering, chemical, electrical, mechanical, and mining, was chosen by the great majority of the students, with a total of one hundred thirty registered; education ranked second, with fifty-six enrolled; letters and sciences third, with thirty-one students; liberal arts fourth, with twenty-eight students registered; while the other fields of study ranged from twenty to one students. There were one hundred fifty-two students whose major subjects were not mentioned.

It is a most encouraging sign to observe the tendency of the modern Filipino youths to choose as their professions the ones that mean most in the economic development of their Country. In 1930, liberal arts, letters and sciences, engineering, education, commerce and agriculture were the most popular courses studied by the students. In 1935, engineering, education, letters and sciences, and liberal arts were the leading courses.

The careers of female students. The students of the female sex are quite few in number, but it is very interesting to observe that some of them are beginning to show promise in various courses of study. This praise is especially given to the two women students in this Country who have invaded the men's realm of business and politics. The majority of them have specialized in the fields of study to which women are expected to give their finest contributions, namely, nursing, home economics, and social service.

The two women students just mentioned were both pensioned by the University of the Philippines. One of the students specialized in political science, and the other in banking.

Of the thirty Filipino women students listed, Table IX shows that nursing leads in popularity with seven registered; home economics followed with an enrollment of three students; and the rest of them with only one or two students enrolled. Four of these students were reported unclassified; two were preparing themselves in music.[3]

The very small enrollment of Filipino women students in the institutions of the Country was surprising, and it was not until Adeva explained in his following statement that one could understand the cause:

> It is not because Filipino girls cannot do the work that most of our boys are doing. It is because they are not accustomed to manual labor and to work for families or in restaurants. And when they come here they have to work, for their parents are not financially able to support them through school. It costs more than twice as much to go to school here as in the Philippines.
> It is inconceivable for a Filipino girl to have the parental home without the company of either of the parents, any of the relatives, or trusted friends. It is a Filipino custom to have a girl chaperoned when she goes out, especially if she goes to a foreign Country. Filipino girls who are in the United States now either have their parents, or brothers, or sisters, or relatives, or trusted friends.[4]

Filipino students are found registered in every class in the different institutions of the Country, i.e., from freshman to doctorate. Many of the students have secured their degrees before leaving for the Western world. The undergraduate students outnumbered the graduate students by a great majority.

Table IX

Number of Filipino Women Students in the
American Institutions, 1926*

Schools or Colleges	Number of Students
Banking	1
Bible Study	1
Economics	1
Education	1
Home Economics	3
Housekeeping	2
Letters, Arts, and Sciences	1
Medicine	2
Music	2
Nursing	7
Pharmacy	1
Political Science	1
Social Service	2
Unclassified	4
Y.W.C.A.	1

*Isidoro R. Collado, ed., "Filipino Women Student in America,"
The Filipino Student Bulletin, 5, April-May, 1926.

FOOTNOTES

[1] Lasker, op. cit., p. 274.

[2] Adeva, loc. cit.

[3] Isideroro R. Callado, ed., "Filipino Women Student in America,"
The Filipino Student Bulletin, 5:2, April-May, 1926.

[4] Manuel A. Adeva, "Filipino Students in the United States," The
Mid-Pacific Magazine, 44:121, August, 1932.

CHAPTER VI

CULTURAL AND SOCIAL STATUS OF THE FILIPINO

STUDENTS IN THE UNITED STATES

The social status of Filipino students on the campuses of American colleges and universities is determined by their relationship to their fellow students. It is also dependent upon the regulations of state institutions, and upon the interest and needs of the individual student.

In undertaking a discussion of this subject no attempt will be made to define every phase of the student's status. The objectives of the problem are met by describing the standards of the student rather than defining it in its phases. The following statements are sufficient to indicate the entire content of this chapter: the principal activities in which the Filipino students are engaged; the attitudes of American students toward Filipino students; the factors which contribute to the difficulty of the English language for him; the effects of the new independence law of the Philippines upon the students in state colleges and universities; and the immigration laws.

Activities of Filipino students. The outcome of the study of certain library researches that were made regarding these sort of activities of the students is concerned, seems to show that the most outstanding groups of activities are the academic or cultural, the social, and the recreational. Each of these activities will be considered individually. The trials and tribulations of the students as well, as their successes and triumphs outside and on the college campuses, will be discussed.

Under the term "academic or cultural activities," will be classified those such as orations, debates, essays, declamations, lectures, forums, operas, and concerts. The Filipino students prefer spending their free time in academic pursuits rather than in social activities. The high price of admission prohibits them from attending, as frequently as they desire, operas, concerts, dramas, and lectures. This is to be greatly regretted.

The students often attend organ recitals either at college or at church. They may listen over the radio to musical programs; others go to concerts at assembly periods. Orations, debates, declamations, and forum discussions are more frequently attended, as they are more reasonable in price. The students are anxious to do all they can to make their education as valuable as possible. They attend and participate in this sort of thing more often than either social or recreational activities. Sometimes they form round-table discussions, organized research and lectures, and the like.

A student of the Central Wesleyan College at Warrenton, Missouri, won the first prize of the annual oratorical contest which was conducted under the auspices of the institution.[1] A contest of the same sort was awarded to a student from the University of Arizona.[2] Still another student at Chapman College was given the first honor in the inter-fraternal college oratorical contest.[3] He represented the Chapman Filipino Circle.

In Washington State College, the Filipino Students have often held a debating contest between the students in several colleges, both in intramural and extramural activities. They made a tour of the churches of Pullman and held religious programs.

The above-mentioned activities, especially orations and declamations, are held every year in honor of their Filipino patriot, Jose Rizal. All of these have as a subject the Filipino hero. The winners of this contest are chosen to deliver their oration and declamation when the program of celebration is held. In addition, at such gatherings, speeches and music selections are rendered.

The social activities will include dances, parties, banquets, and shows. Some Filipino students attend public dance halls; others usually attend gatherings at some friend's home in connection with birthday parties, marriage, and baptismal parties. However, most of them entertain their friends in large groups. Some do not dance, because they do not care for that type of amusement, others because they have no desirable place to go. On the other hand, many of these students never attend because in addition to disliking dancing they have no time to spare.

The Filipino students have many social contacts with American friends and with their own people. Students attending church services often are active in this respect. Generally, they are invited into American homes for tea parties and receptions.

In fact, the great majority of the students wish to go to the theaters more frequently than either dances or parties. They choose shows in preference to the other types of academic life, because they are so much more reasonable in price. They attend shows once or twice a week. If the student is working he does not have much time to go out. If one is a very good scholar, one may be able to devote all one's time sleeping, eating, going to college, and studying.

Many of the students traveled extensively and they know that the conditions in different countries are not as they are represented. The large theaters have a great attraction for them; they enjoy the prologues and music as well as the fine type of shows. However, on the whole, they do not care for the low class of pictures that are shown daily, but they enjoy good ones.

The Filipino Alumni Association of the University of Washington[4] was found in 1929. The social activities of the Association are open both to members and to the public. Organizations, especially missions, often invite a Filipino speaker on subjects about the Philippines or about Filipinos in the United States. The Association will delegate one of its members to speak. By so doing, they not only have an opportunity to come into contact with the American people but they also have an opportunity to have social fellowship with them.

"College Night" is one of the several social activities of the

-35-

Association. It has celebrated its traditional affair annual since it was organized.

The students in the institutions of Illinois enjoy their part as well
as the other students of the Country, and said the following:

The Philippine Illini has had a very important and active part in the
life of Illinois Campus. The most outstanding event in our Club was
the annual Rizal day celebration. At that time we invited all our
friends from the faculty and the student body. We entertained them
with music, stories about our hero, and selections from his poems.
A dance followed the program and was enjoyed by all.[5]

The recreational life of the Filipino students on the campus and outside the school premises is greatly enjoyed by them. In 1930, the students at
the University of Oregon formed an organization under the name of "Las Cas
Filipina." It was recognized and approved by the administration of the institution. In this way the students were able to enjoy the extra curricular activities of the University. They participated in various sports, such as volleyball, basketball, tennis, and boxing.[6] Others engaged in swimming, hiking,
baseball, and fencing. The Washington State college, intramural volleyball
trophy was clinched by the Filipino Club in the institution, where more than
twenty-five fraternities and other teams participated, in the tourney. Never-
the-less, the graduate students are not often able to participate in these
sports, due to the fact that all their time is taken up by their studies.

The Filipino Club of Berkeley gives a dinner-program and a dance
at the beginning of every semester, as a reception in honor of the new members of the Association.

At the international banquet, an annual affair in the Washington
State College, the students rendered a musical program which included the
original compositions of one of the Filipino students in the Institution. The
pleasing symphony of the occasion created much enthusiasm among the music
lovers and made the colorful evening a success.

Other activities in which Filipino students are engaged are those of social organizations and fraternities on the campus. The scholastic standing of the Filipino student Club of the University of Washington, which was organized in 1917, is above the university average; because of that fact, some of its members have been initiated to honorary organizations. They are listed members of Phi Beta Kappa, a national scholastic honorary; Phi Sigma, a national biological research honorary; and the Pi Sigma Alpha, a national political-science honorary.[7] There are several others, namely, the Phi Alpha Gamma Fraternity, Sigma Chi, Phi Sigma Delta, Psi Chi, a national honorary society in psychology, and Epsilon Phi, an honorary English Fraternity. These sororities and fraternities are the so called educational and professional organizations. The Filipino students feel that these organizations are worth while, because they are educational in nature and they provide some social contact for the students.

Other lists of organizations to which the students belong are: Cosmopolitan Club, of Colorado State Teachers College; Filipino Student Association, of Kansas University; Philippine Aero Student Club of New York; Intercollegiate Cosmopolitan Club, in Greater Boston; Student Cabinet of the International House in New York; Philippine-Michigan Club, of the University of Michigan; Cosmopolitan Club, of Denver University; International Club, of Northwestern University of McKinlock Campus; Filipino Club, of Tri-State College of Angola, Indiana; Filipino Nurses Association; International Club, of the University of Wisconsin; and the Philippine Alumni Association of Los Angeles.

The majority of the Filipino students belong to the Cosmopolitan or the International Clubs, because these organizations endeavor to promote a feeling of good will and friendship among the students of all the different nationalities.

Filipino students are particularly interested in reading recent books of philosophy, religion, and psychology, which will aid them to develop culturally. They are also interested in reading current magazines and periodicals dealing with policies and attitudes of the United States with the Far East.

Attitude of American students toward Filipino students. The development of attitudes is one of the significant factors in character education. "The goal of modern character education does not simply involve the attainment of certain bodies of knowledge but are more closely related to the actual behavior of persons in society."[8] It is indeed of great value to know something about the relations of persons of different nationalities and races, especially in the institutions where they live and work together, as to whether or not they are pleasant and mutually satisfying.

In this case the attitude between the American and Filipino students toward one another is to be considered. The result of the study made by Nystrum shows the following comments on Filipino life through education:[9] Forty-eight of the students say the "American colleges promote international friendships," and thirty-two declare that "There is very little race prejudice among American college students." Forty-six report that "In American universities one's race or nationality has no effect on one's grades," and ten testify that "Because of race prejudice among professors it is difficult for a foreign student to graduate from an American university." Fifty-two say that "University professors in America attempt to help foreign students become adjusted," and thirty-three reply that "American universities are very generous in granting scholarships to foreign students." Twenty-one suggest a caste system when they assert that "Foreign students are well treated in America because they are part of the intellectual class." Fifty of the students say that "Americans are very generous in giving foreign students part-time employment while attending school," but fifteen indorse the statement "America believes in social isolation for the foreign students." Twenty-six report that "In America poor students work their way through college and are honored with important positions in the student body," and six charge that "American students have inferior mental ability and resort to dishonest methods to secure good grades in their courses." Twelve say that "As foreign students we should not expect to enter into the social life of Americans," and twenty-three are so favorable to America that they declare "Those foreign students who do not like America should decure their education elsewhere."

Many American students who came from various institutions of the Country where Filipino students are found have been interviewed by the investigator for the purpose of getting information from Americans in order to be able to justify the above statements. After summing up he found that the outcome of his personal contact with them emphasized the fact that majority of the American students expressed the idea that they are friendly and sociable toward the Filipino students. They are glad to have them get an education and enjoy all rights and privileges of any student.

Some of these students pointed out that there is no sign of antagonistic feeling on the part of the American student towards the Filipino students. A sympathetic attitude is continuously growing out of the close relationship existing between these two nations, the Philippines and the United States. Others said that some American students have a closer feeling for the Filipinos than for other Oriental students in the institutions of learning in this Country.

Language difficulties. A foreign accent is one of the most difficult things a Filipino student has to overcome. Difficulty with the English language is a hindrance for many of them in their studies. This handicap is due mainly to the fact that the language of his birth is far removed from the English language. All Filipino students are somewhat handicapped by this obstacle. There are, however, those exceptional students who are fluent in speech and whose written style puts to shame the slangy and careless. It is so hard for the student to eradicate this difficulty that it is liable to become a permanent defect throughout his life.

The Friendly Relations Committees Among Foreign Students speaking of the difficulty of foreigners in the English language states:

The only two institutions among many reporting had no provision for special language help by official courses or by voluntary conversation classes.

One Middle-Western observer reported that confusion in Oriental minds caused by the slang used by an instructor![10]

The difficulty in pronunciation is common to all students, high-school or college, especially to foreign students. By "error in pronunciation" is meant failure to place stress upon the proper syllable of the word, such as stressing the third syllable of word "dic-tion-a-ry" instead of the first, or failure correctly to sound the vowel.

It will be remembered that the term "pronunciation" refers to the stress placed on the syllable of a word and to the sound value given to the vowel. "The two extremes of faulty pronunciations are the careless and provincial on the one hand, and the unusually precise on the other."[11] Common habits of mispronunciation include "sense" for "since," "fur" for "for," "ketch" for "catch," "proGRAM" for "PROgram," "adverTISment" for adVERtisement," and "exQUISite" for "EXquisite."

Another difficulty of the English language to the great majority of Filipino students in this Country as well as other foreign students is that of enunciation. The term "enunciation" in this case is a failure to utter consonants, syllables, or words distinctly. The speech of an individual is futile unless it can be heard, although he may have a clear understanding of, and a very earnest belief in, his message. Enunciation, therefore, has to do largely with being heard. The ideal of the speaker in this respect should be to enunciate so clearly that his hearers may without effort, listen to the remarks, concentrating on the substance rather than on the form of the speech.

A great difficulty for every Filipino student in the colleges and universities of the United States is that of grammar. The term "errors in grammar" used in this respect is in its common connotation. By having such a difficulty, the students are even refused admission to institutions of higher learning. However, special courses for backward students are offered in some of the colleges and universities. Errors in grammar are an individual case rather than racial. A good remedy for the elimination of such difficulty is by the use of a process of segregating the students through different courses of study, in order that they must mingle freely with others, rather than scattering them for group study in classes where they may persist in using their own language. Some ungrammatical habits are so deeply fixed that they are hard to eradicate.

Entrance examination in English for foreign students is one of the requirements for admission in college, in so far as the college Entrance Examination Board is concerned, which states as follows:

> Because of the increased number of foreign students applying to American educational institutions for admission, it has become desirable to save those whose English is inadequate from a long and fruitless journey . . . .
> The purpose of the examination is to assist American universities, colleges and scientific schools in judging the ability of students from foreign lands to undertake with reasonable hope of success college work in the English language. By using this examination the colleges will be in a position to dissuade from a long, expensive fruitless journey students who are certain to be unsuccessful because of an inadequate knowledge of English.[12]

Faulty inflection, which refers to the variation in the pitch of the voice, the fluctuation of the voice sounds above or below the average key, is also difficult for the students.

It is very necessary and should be highly emphasized that foreign students in America must learn the law of inflection and its meaning. The law of inflection according to Shurter is, "when the thought is complete, the voice falls; when the thought is incomplete, the voice rises."[13] The thought and not the form of the sentence is the factor, therefore, determining the inflection. It is misleading to teach that the voice always rises at a comma and always falls at a period.

It is commonly believed that if these students think in complete units their voices will fall at the end of each unit. In other words, some believed that the faulty inflection may be mere habit of voice and not a fault in thinking. The fact remains that some stress is being placed upon the development of the ability of the student to think in terms of sentences containing a complete thought.

Emphasis is one of the major difficulties for Filipino and other nationalities of students. The term "emphasis" signifies the art of vocally expressing the relative importance of the words of a sentence of the sentence as a whole. In any discourse there is a wide difference between the various words of any given sentence and between the various sentences of a given paragraph. The task of the student is to make these important words or sentences stand out in bold relief. This is often observed and very distinctly noticed by people, especially by the professors with whom these students come into contact in their every day college life. Hall, Immel, Dalzell, Rew, and Tanquary, professors of the department of speech at the University of Southern California, and Thompson and McCorkle, professors of English at the same institution, said that the cause of such difficulty of these students is that of provincialism of speech, ie, the constant practice of combining the English language with a dialect. This habit is being formed unconsciously, hence they do not realize that it unfortunately goes a long way toward the incorrect construction of the use of the English language.

A solution of the problem or any indications making it possible to forsee, or even predict, major techniques for the Filipino students to correct faulty construction of sentences, mispronunciation of words, and to eliminate provincialism of speech would be of far-reaching importance and of inestimable value to the students affected, to agree among themselves to strive always to speak English whenever addressing one another, and deliberately to set themselves to the task of learning English, or speaking it upon every occasion in order to steep themselves in American customs and idioms of speech--these would make great progress toward adjusting themselves to cultural life in America.

Not only does the mastery of English add to the assurance, security, and confidence of the students, but it affords an inward satisfaction and adds genuine pleasure in being able to understand and appreciate most of what is read or heard. Hence, the English language consciously or unconsciously becomes a potential factor in personal adjustment.

Effects of the new independence law. The passage of the McDuffie-Tydings bill for the independence of the Philippines and the approval of the Repatriation Act were effective in 1934, placing the Filipinos under a quota basis of fifty, as a minimum for students or non-students, because the Islands shall be considered as a separate Country and their people shall be considered aliens.

The former Governor-General of the Philippine Islands, Frank Murphy, in a speech delivered on November 15, 1935, the day when the inauguration of the Philippine Commonwealth Constitution was celebrated as a basis for her complete and absolute independence after a ten-year transition period said:

Under the stipulation of the Tydings-McDuffie Act, by voting the adoption of this constitution, the Filipino people themselves definitely and freely decided the matter of independence. This act was fundamentally a product of the political idealism and unselfishness of the American people. It was the generous act of a generous people . . . the Filipino have definitely, and gladly assumed the conditions and responsibilities and have adhered to the course that leads ultimately to full sovereignty and independence. [14]

Ever since this law became effective, the Filipino students attending the State Universities of the Country are required to pay tuition fees. This adds to their serious problems due to the lack of financial support, which prevents them from continuing their studies. As a consequence, the enrollment of Filipino students in these institutions is greatly reduced.

Rigid residence requirements are believed to have caused the sharp decline in the number of Filipino students enrolled this semester at the Berkeley branch of the University of California. Only 34 Filipinos are registered there now as against 67 last year.

Uncertainty of their status under the present law and economic difficulties are also held responsible for the decline.[15]

As soon as the term of ten years has elapsed, the Filipinos will be classified as one with the Chinese and Japanese under the stigmas of the exclusion acts. There will be a tendency in the years to come that they as students cannot be employed while in a university in any kind of job that will be one that an American could fill as is now being done to other Orientals.

On Section 14 of the McDuffie-Tydings bill regarding the immigration of Filipinos to the United States after independence will be fully granted, states that "Upon the final and complete withdrawal of American sovereignty over the Philippines the immigration laws of the United States shall apply to persons who were born in the Philippine Islands to the same extent as in the case of other foreign Countries.

FOOTNOTES

[1] Juan Collas, ed., The Filipino Student Bulletin, 4:2, June, 1927.

[2] Ibid., p. 9.

[3] Honesto A. Villanueva, ed., Commonwealth Chronicle, 2:4, January 1, 1936.

[4] Adeva, op. cit., p. 123.

[5] Collas, op. cit., p. 14.

[6] Manuel A. Adeva, ed., The Filipino Student Bulletin, 12:4, April-May, 1934.

[7]Manuel A. Adeva, ed., The Filipino Student Bulletin, 9:5, November, 1931.

[8]Nystrum, op. cit., p. 149.

[9]Ibid., p. 152.

[10]Wheeler, King, Davidson, op. cit., p. 155.

[11]Edwin D. Shurter, Public Speaking (New York: Allyn and Bacon, 1903), p. 27.

[12]School and Society, "Examinations in English of Foreign Students by the College Entrance Examination Board," 33:165, January-June, 1931.

[13]Shurter, op. cit., p. 59.

[14]Frank Murphy, Philippines Free Press, 29:47, November 23, 1935.

[15]B. T. Olivera, ed., "California List of Students Drops," The Filipino Student Bulletin, 14:1, January, 1936.

CHAPTER VII

CONTRIBUTION OF FILIPINO STUDENTS

A race, like an individual, becomes a highly civilized and useful in proportion as it learns to use the good things of this earth, not as an end but as a means toward promoting its own moral and religious growth and the prosperity and happiness of the world.

This chapter has been written to show in a concrete way the progressive methods and ideas of the Filipino students in this Country. It is interesting to observe the scope of their services and constructive work being carried on in several ways.

The important contributions of the Filipino youth in the United States are those things which are experienced and absorbed into his personality and capability. Whatever is needed by way of education and experience to prepare young individuals for improvement and progress is desirable. That which an individual student sees in a situation, which directs his attention upon certain factors, is largely a product of his underlying preconceptions and beliefs. The influence of good of such gatherings is very manifest. The teaching of conferences are disseminated widely for the benefit of the students who attend certain occasions.

To determine the kind of contributions a Filipino student can give towards the public, such as institutions, conferences, and others, is the main object of investigation and discussion of this chapter.

Disseminating ideas about the Philippines. Students of the Filipino race are very proud to disperse certain notions about their Country, the Philippine Islands. Such conceptions will be gained through publicity in newspapers, magazines, and bulletins. Some other sources by which it could be spread are through classroom reports by the students, through speeches, orations, open-forum discussions, debates, and in public gatherings, such as conferences.

Important subjects are specially selected in this connection, e.g., "Lincoln and Filipino Aspirations," "The Rise and Fall of the Filipino Nation,"[1] and "The economic Reconstruction in the Philippines."[2] To the latter one has been specifically emphasized the rise of agricultural industries, due to the fact that modern and scientific methods were introduced. Still another factor is that of her domestic and foreign commerce. "The Young Men Christian Association in the Philippines,"[3] and "Speaking of the World's 'Y' Conference,"[4] were among the several speeches of Filipinos delivered on August 9, 1931, at the Twentieth World Conference of the Y.M.C.A., held in Cleveland, Ohio. It has been conveyed to the public the progress and outlook of the Association among the people who are the inheritors of the culture and civilization of the Orient enriched by the impacts of two civilizations from the Occident, the latin and Anglo-Saxon; the people who are essentially homogeneous racially and religiously; the people who in their effort to achieve an independent existence are seeking to develop their national life upon Christian foundations, solid and enduring. The Association itself has something to do with the strategic position of the Philippines in the oriental scheme of life; the enthusiastic support of the inhabitants of the islands, because of its materialistic and without selfish ends to serve; it is highly beneficial in engendering the proper spirit of competitive service among different institutions of uplift; and it gives opportunity to contribute to the solution of international and inter-racial relations.

"In Defense of the Philippines"[5] is an article which challenges the charge previously used against the capacity of the Filipinos. It states that "they will be torn apart by lingual, religious and racial differences." Ideas about the Country and its people are emphasized point for point to give distinct and accurate information as to its truth.

An oration[6] about the Philippines, delivered at the University of Arizona by a Filipino student, has predicted that freedom and independence should be granted immediately to the more than thirteen million souls, in order that America's moral obligation should fulfill per promise to the people of the Islands. Certain strong motives were pointed out to justify the fact that the land of promise is prepared for liberty.

Still other subjects which diffused the thoughts about the Country are these: "Facts About the Philippines,"[7] which stressed the idea that the percentage of literacy can be favorably compared with most of the independent nations of the World, that in fact, the proportion of those who can read and write in the Philippine Islands is higher than that of any of the Countries of North America, some of Europe, and some other countries in the world.

Representing the Filipino race in conferences. It is a great opportunity and privilege for the Filipino students to attend conferences and institutes. They learn many things which they can preserve in mind to convey to their people in the Philippines as well as those who are not able to go. This is the proper place to praise the great idea of those people who started inviting the youth for the conferences. These conferences are very nice, interesting, and instructive. The students could surely acquire very valuable experience, and they will hope to start similar things among the young children of their own, by the time they are back in their homeland.

They are glad to form new and pleasant friendships with different people of different nationalities that they are longing to meet, and to join the international group, where they have their discussions and acquaintances. Besides the many inspirations that could be seen they have also wonderful rest and relaxation at the conference.

The objects of these conferences are: (1) to create a sense of unity and co-operation, pervading the student atmosphere with the spirit of oneness and interdependence; (2) to provide an opportunity for the study of human relations and for the change of points of view between oriental and occidental students, as well as the students of various other countries, to the end of that fellowship based on intelligent understanding of the problems facing the orient and occident may be established; (3) to act as missionaries from the Philippines, bringing to these conferences the message and contribution of the life and culture of their people; and (4) to experience the rich spiritual nurture and catch a vision of social service, which are in the very atmosphere of these conferences.

One of the Filipino student representatives to these conferences says the following:

> The remarkable personalities who attend it, together with the winter scenic beauty of the place made the conference a very significant one . . . Attending conferences of this kind will give one important knowledge 'which gives to life its values, perspective, moral judgments, dynamic resources, and true sense of the spiritual essence of the universe.'
>
> It is my great hope to see that many of our Filipino students in America can find an opportunity to attend at least one of these intercollegiate conferences before returning to the Philippines. This in addition to already acquired 'treasures' abroad will help them formulate within themselves a sound and constructive Filipino Christian philosophy of life.[8]

The various conferences, national, oriental, and summer conferences, are held everywhere in the Country; the following is the list with the dates and places where they are held: The National conferences consisted of the Student Volunteer Movement, Indianapolis, Indiana, December 28, 1935-January 1, 1936;[9] Buffalo, New York, December 30, 1931-January 3, 1932; the Twentieth World Conference of the Y.M.C.A. in Cleveland, Ohio, August 4-9, 1931; and the International Convention,[10] held at the Rotary Club, Chicago, December, 1935.

The Oriental conferences constituted the Foreign Students Convention, Madison, Wisconsin, February 22-25, 1934; and the Oriental Christian

Federation Conference, New York City, New York, March 29, 1934.

The Summer conferences are held once a year, and in 1926 were composed of the following:[11]

Hollister, Missouri, June 4-14; Seaback, Washington, June, 12-20; Eagles Mere, Pa., June 11-12; Lake Geneva, Wisconsin, June 15-25; Blue Ridge, North Carolina, June 15-25; Northfield, Massachusetts, June 16-24; Estes Park, Colorado, August 24-September 3; Blairstown, New Jersey, June 26-July 1st.

The conferences held in 1927 were:[12] Tougaloo College, Mississippi, May 27-June 3; Kings Mountain, North Carolina, June 3-13; Geneva, Wisconsin, June 10-20; Seaback Washington, June 11-19; Northfield, Massachusetts, June 15-23; Blue Ridge, North Carolina, June 17-26; Blairstown, New Jersey, June 25-30; Hollister, Missouri, June 7-17; Eagles Mere, Pa., June 14-24; and Estes Park, Colorado, August 24-September 2.

In these conferences, the youth shall be guided actually to perform the duties and tasks they are supposed to perform.

They shall learn how to eliminate race prejudice and discriminations of race or color; they shall try to reconcile religion and science and employ both as servants and not their quarrelling matters; they may seek to do away with capitalism and equitably distribute the goals of this work among the children of men; and they will try to make this a new world--just, peaceful, loving, and a veritable democracy of God.

Success of Filipino students in American colleges and universities.
In the State University of Montana, a Filipino student[13] in the Department of Fine Arts became an Art editor of the 1934 "Sentinel," a university year book. He was so interested that he prepared many wonderful designs and drawings for its elaboration. One of the professors in the department says that the student "shows promise and will undoubtedly make a name for himself when he returns home."

Manuel Franco,[14] at the University of Washington, is a poet and an

-50-

author whose poetry were published in a book by the Henry Harrison Publisher Company of New York, containing fifty-three original poems. Besides this volume, he contributed five poems in the American Anthology of Poetry, a lyric, entitled "A Reverie" was published by a music publisher in the East, and another lyric "Silver Stars, was sent to Hollywood, California.

Januario Puruganan,[15] at the College of Wooster, Ohio published in book form his poem, entitled "To Mother and Other Poems." Other poems were recorded in the Wooster Voice, the college weekly paper.

A student of exceptional ability in writing poems at the University of Southern California, Alfonso P. Santos,[16] has published his book of poems, "A Garland of Sampaguitas, or Flowers of Melancholy." He is at present a member of the senior class with the Epsilon Phi distinction an honorary English Fraternity. Several of his best lyrics are "Spring," "Fragrance of Ylang-Ylang Flowers," "Parting," "Remembering," and "Moonlight in a Dream."

Primo E. Quevedo,[17] another student of the same institution, published a pamphlet, entitled "Read the Truth About Hilario C. Moncado." Many copies of the pamphlet were sent to different parts of the world, all over the United States, Hawaii, the Philippines, and other places.

Marcario Z. Landicho[18] became a member of the editorial staff of the "Daily Illini," official student newspaper of the University of Illinois. He was editor of the Filipino Community Press, and possesses and unusual faculty for writing English.

A Government student, Ciriaco Coronel,[19] who attended the Massachusetts Institute of Technology, invented a device known as the Electromagnetic Pick-up for radio phonograph, which has been patented.

A noted Filipino sculptor, Apolinario E. Zoleta,[20] made sponge busts of President Franklin D. Roosevelt, George Washington, Abraham Lincoln, and Thomas Edison. He was awarded a medal when the busts were exhibited at the World's Fair, in Chicago, in 1933. The sculptor attended the

Chicago Art Institute for a year before he secured employment at the American-Greek Sponge Company in the City.

S. P. Aguinaldo, a student at the music department of Washington State College in Pullman, has composed a symphony for full orchestra of the institution, entitled "Filipinas." The piece of music was presented to Robert Nelson, an assistant professor of organ and theory who says:

> He deserves high credit for having brought to successful completion so ambitious a work. Few people realize the immense amount of labor involved in the writing and scoring of a symphony. The mechanical work alone of copying parts for the many orchestral instruments is appalling and yet this is only the last step in the writing process. It is extremely rare for an undergraduate in an American college or university to attempt a composition in the symphonic form and this fact, coupled with the inventive fertility and technical command displayed in the present instance, make Mr. Aguinaldo's essay most exceptional.[21]

Another talented student, Rudolfo R. Cornejo of the Chicago Musical College, presented a number of his compositions with those from foreign masters at a piano recital held at the International House, Chicago, under the auspices of the Institute of Oriental Students. He is so gifted as a pianist and composer that he was awarded the La Violette Scholarship in Composition and won a scholarship in piano under Glenn Dillard Gunn of the college. The Director of the Chicago Musical College says of Cornejo:

> I consider him to be an unusually gifted young man who has a chance to go far in his profession. His diligence, his courage, his charming personality, will all help to make this promise a fulfillment.[22]

FOOTNOTES

[1] Manuel A. Adeva, ed., The Filipino Student Bulletin, 8:3, December-January, 1930-31.

[2] Conrado O. Santa Romana, "The Economic Reconstruction in the Philippines," The Filipino Student Bulletin, 13:3, November, 1934.

[3] Camilo Osias, "The Y.M.C.A. in the Philippines," The Filipino Student Bulletin, 9:4, October 15, 1931.

[4] Ibid., p. 5.

[5] Francisco A. Delgado, "In Defense of the Philippines," The Filipino Student Bulletin, 14:1-3, December, 1935.

[6] Collas, ed. loc. cit.

[7] Adeva, ed., loc. cit.

[8] Manuel A. Adeva, ed., The Filipino Student Bulletin, 12:1, April-May, 1934.

[9] B.T. Olivera, ed., The Filipino Student Bulletin, 14:2, December, 1935.

[10] Honesto A. Villaneuva, ed., Commonwealth Chronicle, December 15, 1935.

[11] Collado, ed. op. cit., p. 7.

[12] Collas, ed., op. cit., p. 19.

[13] Adeva, ed., op. cit., p. 3.

[14] Loc cit.

[15] Op. cit.

[16] Tom Lawless, ed., Southern California Daily Trojan, February, 1936.

[17] Manuel A. Adeva, ed., The Filipino Student Bulletin, 8:3, December-January, 1930-31.

[18] Pablo S. Katigbak, ed., The Filipino Student Bulletin, 7:5, December, 1929.

[19] Adeva, ed., loc. cit.

[20]Ibid., p. 2.

[21]Manuel A. Adeva, ed., The Filipino Student Bulletin, 10:4, June, 1933.

[22]Ibid., p. 4.

CHAPTER VIII

OCCUPATIONAL OUTLOOK OF FILIPINO STUDENTS

Thousands of citizens of the philippines formerly were students in the United States of America, and they cherish the most genuine affection for American people and institutions. A great many of these Filipino students have already returned to their Country, where they are now engaged in the occupational procedure of promoting and improving commerce, education, industry, philanthropy, public health, religion and other interests among their own people. They constitute the most valuable means of communication and fellowship between America and the Philippines.

The American people who have become friendly with the students have been greatly broadened in outlook. There are few school boys or girls in this Country who have not a more intelligent appreciation of the Filipino culture through contact with representative students from the Islands. The earnest efforts of these students have had a marked effect on America's newer policies towards them, but more students are still in this Country struggling for existence on the rough road to their ultimate ends.

In the United States. It is a great satisfaction to note that the outlook for achievement among the Filipino students in the United States is most encouraging. Many have definitely arrived and are making a creditable showing. They hold positions of different categories, such as instructors, physicians, ministers, commissioners, teachers, laboratory assistants, and the like.

A student, Higinio Mendoza, who obtained the degree of Doctor of Medicine, became a resident physician of the West Philadelphia Homeopathic Hospital while in the United States. M. J. David,[1] formerly from Chicago, is now practicing in the City of Los Angeles. He had been an interne at the

Queen of the Angels Hospital before he established his office here. Jose Zialcita y Cailles has also been a successful Filipino physician in America. Simeon Tiopaco was an interne of the Cook County Hospital.

Francisco A. Delgado is at present the new Philippine Resident Commissioner in the United States. He was formerly a member of the House of Representatives of the Philippine Legislature when he was appointed to his new post. The Commissioner was a government pensionado who acquired his education at Yale and Indiana Universities.

Pedro T. Orata is the only Filipino instructor in the Department of Education at Ohio State University. Fidel Del Rosario was a fellow of the Rockefeller Foundation while he was taking his Doctor of Science degree in medicine at Johns Hopkins University. One of the laboratory assistants in the Forest Products Laboratory, of the United States Department of Agriculture, at Madison, has been Mariano P. Ramiro. He has also been working on the quantitative determination of cellulosic material by absorption and X-ray defraction.

Priscilla Carinio is an assistant teacher in the kindergarten training school at Oakton Public School, Evanston, Illinois. She was graduated from the National College of Education of the City. Eugenio Resos is a draftsman at the Boeing Airplane Company in Seattle; and Manuel Rustia is working with the Philippine Commercial Attache in New York City.

The minister of the Filipino First Christian Church of Los Angeles is Felix Pascua, who succeeded Silvestre Norales. Pascua is at present taking post graduate work at the University of Southern California, specializing in religion. The Reverend Vicente A. Zambra has been a pastor of the Filipino Presbyterian Church at Stockton.

In the Philippine Islands. A large majority of the students have returned to the Islands to take up their life work after receiving an education in the United States. They are looked up to by their fellow-countrymen, for everyone of them is holding the key to proficiency in any line of endeavor.

In 1921-1922, there were many students who obtained their doctorates in this country. Before they came to America, some of them were Fellows from the University of the Philippines; others were Government employees. All of these students were sent by the Government of the Islands, and were the following:[2] Leopoldo B. Ulchanco was a product of Harvard University who secured the degree of Doctor of Philosophy in Zoology. He was graduated from the College of Agriculture, University of the Philippines, where he was an instructor in economic entomology and editor-in-chief of the college magazine when appointed to a government fellowship in the United States in 1919. As soon as he returned to the Islands, he followed the same line of work on the staff of the college of Agriculture at the University of the Philippines.

Encarnacion Alzona received her Doctor of Philosophy in history from Columbia University. She took her place in the public institutions which the United States helped to organize in the Philippines. Alzona is at present an assistant professor of history in the University of the Philippines. Her achievements not only indicate the fallacy of questioning the mental capacity of the Filipinos, but even more strikingly exemplify the great advance made by Filipino women during the past twenty-four years of American administration and of increasing Filipino education.

Two among these Students were F. M. Frondo and V. Villegas, who specialized in animal husbandry. On both of them were conferred the Doctor of Philosophy in Agriculture, and they are now teaching in the College of Agriculture at Los Banos, in the Islands.

Other degrees were granted to Regino G. Padua and Rufino Abriol, by Johns Hopkins University. They were conferred the degrees of Doctor of Public Health. The two physicians had secured their degrees of Doctor of Tropical Medicine, before leaving Manila to the States. Padua is now connected with the Philippine Bureau of Public Health, while Abriol is again with the United States Quarantine Service at Manila. Prior to his arrival at Johns Hopkins, he was detailed at the United States Quarantine offices at San Francisco, Boston, Philadelphia, and Baltimore, and at the immigration offices at Angel and Ellis islands.

Jorge Bocobo,[3] Former Dean of the College of Law at the University of the Phillipines, became president of that institution. He was graduated from the University of Indiana where he secured his Bachelor of Laws degree in 1907. He was among the first Government pensionado students in the United States in 1903. In the Islands, he worked as a law clerk in the Executive Bureau until 1910. Later he was made a professor in the University of the Philippines, where he became Dean of the department of law, in 1916. Recently in 1930, the University of Southern California conferred to him the honorary degree of Doctor of Laws.

Pablo N. Mabbun is a member of the faculty of the University of the Philippines. He obtained the degree of Doctor of Philosophy in agricultural economics from the University of Wisconsin.

A student who secured with honors the degree of Doctor of Philosophy in geology and mineralogy from the University of Chicago in 1923, is now the head of the department of geology in the state university. He accepted a fellowship offered him by the American Scientific Society, and was the first of his race to be honored by the distinguished body, and only man of recognized ability and accomplishments have in the past merited the society's fellowship. He came back to the United States to assume the new position offered him.

Carlos P. Romulo[4] was one of the Filipino delegates to the International Convention held at the Rotary Club in Chicago on December, 1935. He graduated from Columbia University. He is now the head of a newspaper syndicate in the Philippines. In 1916, he was a reporter, and then became editor of the Manila Herald, later the Mahila Tribune. He was made managing editor of the T-V-T publications.

A student in aviation, Procopio N. Laurel,[5] was graduated from the

Chicago Aviation School in Chicago, Illinois. Shortly after finishing his course, he attended the Candron Military School of Aviation at Le Crotoy, Somme, France, in 1920. Following, he served at the German Air Company at Staaken, Berlin. Returning to the Philippine Islands, he joined the Philippine Aerial Taxi Company as pilot and assistant chief mechanic, from 1930-1932. At the present time, he is one of the instructors of the Valeriano Aviation College.

Celedonio Ancheta, Marcos Hernando, Silvestre Morales, Marcos Berbano, Ted Sumabat, Vicenta Jamias[6] and David Gilito were all products of the University of Southern California, and are now at home engaged in the teaching profession. Some of them are teaching in the high schools; others are assistant professors in colleges and universities in the City of Manila and other small cities in the Islands. Ancheta received his Master of Arts degree in history and also attended the University of California at Berkeley before he came to this institution. While there he was commissioned as First Lieutenant. Now, he is teaching in one of the high schools in Manila, but he is expecting to occupy a high military position in the newly established Philippine Army and Navy. On Hernando was conferred the degree of Master of Arts in political science. He was an alumnus of the State Teachers College in San Diego. He is connected with a private institution in the Philippines.

Morales and Berbano were granted the degrees of Master of Arts in Sociology. They took their undergraduate work at Chapman College, which was formerly called the California Christian College, before they came to the University. The former has established an institution of his own, where the latter is employed as one of the members of the faculty.

Sumabat and Janias secured the degrees of Bachelor of Arts in English. A year later, Sumabat went to Notre Dame University and received his Master of Arts in the same subject. He is now a member of the faculty of the Far Eastern University, at Manila. Janias was the only Filipino woman student ever attended the University of Southern California. She is at present an assistant professor of English at the National University of the Philippines. Gilito is also holding a position in the teaching field. He received his Master of Science degree in Education at the University.

Gerardo Espejo who obtained his Doctor of Medicine from the College of Medical Evangelist at Loma Linda, has been in the Islands for quite a while. He is working in the General Hospital of the Philippines since his return. He also attended the College of Medicine at the University of Southern California.

Antonio P. Alvir[7] went to America after having obtained his Bachelor's degree in the College of Liberal Arts, University of the Philippines. He took his post-graduate work at the University of Chicago. He was awarded the degree of Master of Science, in 1921. After several years of hard labor, he was given his Ph. D. degree in mining, and returned to the Islands immediately. There he joined the Bureau of Science, where he served as geologist for six successive years. He also attended the Colorado School of Mines in Golden, Colorado, in 1917, following his arrival to this Country.

Jose Santiago[8] who worked extensively for his Master of Arts degree at Columbia University has recently returned to the Philippines where he was made professor of the Philippine Women's University.

Jose A. Ozamis[9] received his Master of Laws degree at Columbia University, after he took his Bachelor of Laws degree from the University of the Philippines, in 1916. Returning to the Islands, he practiced law. As a result of a plebiscite in his home town, he was appointed by the provincial governor of his province on December 19, 1929. When that term of office expired in 1931 he was elected representative of Occidental, Misamis, with an overwhelming majority over his opponents. In the same post, he was re-elected in the 1934 elections; at the present time, he is chairman of the important committee on the revision of laws in that Country.

Angel Arguelles[10] was also among the first Filipino Government pensionados to the United States. He specialized in agricultural chemistry at the University of Illinois and there he received the degree of Bachelor of Science. He was appointed by the Governor-General of the Philippines to a new post as Assistant Director of the Bureau of Science after his return to the Philippines.

Other students who are now holding responsible positions in the islands are:[11] Victorio Edades, Professor of Arts at the University of Santo Tomas, Manila; Pedro Guiang, Statistician in the Bureau of Education; Angel Instrella, Principal of Samar High School; Teifilo De Juan, Cashier of a National Bank in Manila; Jose Montilla, Fish Expert in the Bureau of Science; Vicente O. Navea, Contractor and publisher; Maria Orosa, Chief of Food Division in the Bureau of Science of the Philippines; Agustin Palacal, Editor of the New Katipunan, Manila; Amos F. Rudolfo, Chief of one division in the Philippine Bureau of Forestry; Nasario Penas, manager of a big lumber company in the Islands; Florencio Tameses, Assistant Director of Forestry; and Nicanor Tomas, Manager of Peoples Bank and Trust Company, Laguna.

Opportunities of Government and private students for procuring all types of positions. The possibility of opportunities for the students to obtain their positions in the Philippines rely upon their classifications, whether a pensionado or a private student. There are certain conclusions that could be drawn concerning the effects of specific rules and regulations particularly applied to both students.

In public firms, the government student is necessarily given the first preference, because of his scholarship contract of serving the Philippine Government one and one-half years for every year of his scholarship, before the private student is assured to a position. These students are subject to pass the civil-service examinations[12] prior to the approval of one's assignment, especially the teaching profession. These examinations became effective on September 1, 1903. Their definite purpose was to make "requisite for eligibility for promotion of those already in the service or of entrance for those seeking admission."

The effects of this after several months of effectiveness was that there was a considerable amount of misunderstanding of the conditions accompanying the change and a consequent antagonistic ideas about it. As the gain in impartiality of treatment became apparent, this ill-feeling of the individual concerned was gradually changed until now a general satisfaction appears to prevail on the part of the teaching force with reference to the change.

The most just criticism of teachers as to the conduct of this office of Insular Government was the difference of treatment accorded teachers in the matter of compensation, leave and absence by reason of sickness. But the danger of such discrimination was entirely removed by the passage of the force under the ordinary regulations governing the service.

The influence of political pull must be considered by private students as to the possibility of obtaining positions in the teaching field and other affairs. It is remarkable at all times, due to the fact that politics in the Islands is taken seriously and followed with vigour by politicians as well as those higher up.

The appointment of all government student aspirants to such positions must also be made on merit,[13] so that the Philippine Government recommended "that obligation of making return by hearty and conscientious service be kept constantly before the students benefited." The term "merit" in this case is the characteristic which should be rewarded, and an urgent need in the teaching field in the Philippines today as well as in the United States of America is a measuring instrument or a method of measurement which would be exactly ascertain the merit of the individual teacher. Under the terms of the law, those students may take not more than sixty days of vacation after their arrival in Manila and are then under obligation to accept appointment in a suitable position in the government service and to enter appropriate civil-service examinations to secure eligibility for regular appointment.

The private student is especially favored for selection to employment in the private institutions with placement according to his major field of interest. Various private concerns in the Philippines are anxious to choose those who graduated from the recognized institutions in the United States. A private student with his valuable experience is not afraid of work and he is willing to accept most any kind of position offered him. The pensionado student cannot possibly obtain a position in private pursuits, unless he resigns his scholarship pledge from the government or institution which awarded him aids for his education.

FOOTNOTES

[1] Honesto A. Villanueva, ed., Commonwealth Chronicle, January 1, 1936.

[2] W.W. Marquardt, "Filipino Students in the United States," School and Society, 16:440-42, July-December, 1922.

[3] R. McCulloch Dick, ed., "New President of U.P.," Philippine Free Press, 28:4, August 18, 1934.

[4] Honesto A. Villanueva, ed., Commonwealth Chronicle, December 14, 1935.

[5] R. McCulloch Dick, ed., "First Filipino Gets Commercial License," Philippines Free Press, 29:34, November 9, 1935.

[6] Villanueva, ed., loc. cit.

[7] A.C. Fabian, ed., "Who is Who in the Philippines," Graphic, (September 27, 1934), p. 22.

[8] Ibid., p. 51.

[9] R. McCulloch Dick, ed., "Thumbnail Sketches of Legislators," Philippines Free Press, 28:30, September 14, 1934.

[10] Ibid., p. 38.

[11] Adeva, op. cit., p. 123.

[12] Fourth Annual Report of the General Superintendent of Education (Manila: Bureau of Public Printing, September 1904), p. 26.

[13] Ibid., p. 27.

CHAPTER IX

SUMMARY

The technique used was chiefly to make an attempt to obtain available published materials through library research to which the problem is related. Never-the-less, endeavors have been made to secure personal interviews with students. The materials gained have covered the following fields of interest: the historical background of Filipino students in the United States, the classification of the students, their geographical distribution, the student's educational interests, their status in the Country, their contribution, and their occupational outlook.

History of the Filipino student movement in the United States. Ever since the United States drew from Spain her sovereign power over the Philippine Islands, Filipino students have arrived within her boundaries. The Philippine government began to send students in 1903. They were required to stay for a period of four or more years of study, according to the Philippine Legislative Act of 1924. Their ages ranged from sixteen to twenty years. There was a tremendous increase of these students year after year, especially during 1919. This movement was greatly increased by the private students in later years.

Financial resources of Filipino students. Filipino students in this Country consist chiefly of three different types: namely, the pensionado students who are supported by the government, institutions, and others; the wholly self-supporting students who earn all their expenses while attending college, besides burning the "mid-night oil" to obtain the desired education; and the partially self-supporting students who are the recipients of financial resources from their parents, relatives, or friends.

The percentage of each of these groups, according to Mystrum, is 63 per cent for the entirely self-supporting students, and 25 per cent earn about 75 per cent of their expenses, while 12 per cent earn 50 per cent or less for the partially self-supporting students. The report of the Friendly Relations Committees Among Foreign Students shows 9.8 per cent for the pensionado students; 87.3 per cent for the wholly self-supporting students; and 2.9 per cent of the partially self-supporting ones.

Geographical distribution of Filipino students in America. Students from the Philippines are distributed into three geographical divisions in this Country, the Eastern, the Middle-western, and the Western sections.

At the colleges and universities in the Eastern section in 1929-1930, there was a total of one hundred thirty-nine, and seventy-three in 1934-1935. In the institutions of the Middle-western section is found an unusually large group of students. In 1929-1930, there were two hundred seventy-seven, and in 1934-1935, one hundred twenty-one students. The schools in the Western section of the Country had the largest population of Filipino students, with a total of four hundred eighty in 1929-1930 and three hundred fifty-four in 1934-1935.

Favorable climatic conditions, a low tuition fee, the influence of a brother, friend, or a relative and some others are certain factors which attracted their attention, and thus, made the distribution uneven. The results of the investigation indicate that 10 per cent are attending the Eastern colleges and universities; thirty-four per cent are found in the Middle-western institutions; and fifty-six per cent in the Western schools.

Major Educational interests of Filipino students. The Filipinos have indicated their major interests in various fields of endeavor, ranging from agriculture to zoology. A great majority of the students show rich promise in their selected vocations and fields of study.

Liberal Arts, letters and sciences, engineering, education,

commerce, and agriculture are the most popular courses among the students. This is a most encouraging sign of the tendency of the modern generation of the Islands to take up those professions that are valuable in the economic development of the Philippines.

Cultural and social status of the Filipino students in the United States. The status of the Filipino students in the institutions of learning have been varied. Their activities in the campus are divided into several programs; cultural, social, and recreational. The cultural activities include orations, essays, declamations, lectures, forums, operas, and concerts; under social are found dances, parties, banquets, and shows; and recreational covers baseball, volleyball, basketball, tennis, boxing, swimming, hiking, and fencing.

The students prefer spending their free time in cultural pursuits rather than in social activities, because of the high price of admission to the latter. This prohibited them from attending, as often as they desire, operas, concerts, lectures and dramas.

The language difficulties of the students consist of foreign accent, pronunciation, enunciation, grammar, inflection, and emphasis.

There is a very distinct effect of the new independence law of the Philippines upon the Filipino students in the United States, especially those who are attending the State universities. The enrollment in the institutions is gradually decreasing because of the change.

Contribution of Filipino students. The contributions of the Filipino students in America are many. Selected subjects about the Philippines could be spread through speeches in conferences, publicity, forum discussions, debates, and orations.

The students contribute many things in the institutions where they attend, and in other public places of the Country. Some become editors of the institutions' daily papers; several are musicians who compose symphonies and compositions to be used for the orchestras on college campuses; others write poems and lyrics; others invent; and still others are sculptors.

Occupational outlook of Filipino students. The returned students in the Philippine Islands, as well as those who are still in the mainland of the United States, are holding responsible positions. Several students of this Country are physicians, instructors, laboratory assistants, ministers, commissioners, fellows, assistant teachers, and draftsmen.

Many are holding the key to proficiency in any line of endeavor in the Philippines at the present time. Such positions are the following: instructors, physicians, Governmental officials, geologists, statisticians, bankers, contractors, and publishers, economists, editors, lumbermen, forestry, and several other employments held by them.

Conclusion. The influence of the student's movement is of intense significance. Their presence in this Country adds directly to the broadening influence of whatever American institutions they attend and makes new points of contact for American students. This makes for better personal understanding between Americans and Filipinos and lessens the danger of future international misunderstandings. It inclines the Filipino students upon their return to continue to think America, and they will never fail to stress the importance of having been so dealt with that they have become familiar with American ways, which they have learned to appreciate.

The Filipino students on the whole are serious, eager, and earnest, generous in their contacts with Americans as well as with other races.

The wholly-self-supporting student has shown with what great difficulties the Filipino students in the United States must struggle for their college education.

BIBLIOGRAPHY

A. BOOKS

Alzona, Encarnacion. History of Education in the Philippines, 1565–1930. Manila: University of the Philippines Press, 1930. 273 pp.

Berbano, Marsos P. The Social Status of the Filipinos in Los Angeles County. Department of Sociology, University of Southern California, August, 1930.

Catapusan, Benicio. The Filipino Occupational and Recreational Activities in Los Angeles. Department of Sociology, University of Southern California, February, 1934.

Lasker, Bruno. Filipino Immigration. Chicago: The University of Chicago Press, 1931. 437 pp.

Shurter, Edwin D. Public Speaking. New York: Allyn and Bacon, 1903. 27–59 pp.

Wheeler, Reginald W., King, Henry H., and Davidson, Alexander B., editors. The Foreign Students in America. Commission on Survey of Foreign Students in the United States of America. New York: Association Press, 1925. 17, 151–159 pp.

B. DIRECTORY

Adeva, Manuel A., editor. Directory of Filipino Students in the United States. New York City: 1934–1935.

C. PERIODICAL ARTICLES

Adeva, Manuel A., editor. "Filipino Students in the United States," The Filipino Students Bulletin, 8:12, May-June, 1931.

_____. "Honor Student at the University of Washington," The Filipino Student Bulletin, 9:4–5, November, 1931.

_____. "Worthy of Emulation," The Filipino Student Bulletin, 8:2, March 1931.

Adeva, Manuel A. The Filipino Student Bulletin, 8:2-3, December-January, 1930-1931.

_____. The Filipino Student Bulletin, 12:1-3, April-May, 1934.

_____. The Filipino Student Bulletin, 8:3, February, 1931.

_____. The Filipino Student Bulletin, 13:2, December, 1934.

_____. The Filipino Student Bulletin, 7:3, January-February, 1930.

_____. The Filipino Student Bulletin, 10:4, June, 1933.

_____. "The Filipino Student in the United States," The Mid-Pacific Magazine, 44:119-123. August, 1932.

Collado, Isidoro R., editor. "Filipino Women Students in America," The Filipino Student Bulletin, 5:2, and 7, April-May, 1926.

Collas, Juan, editor. The Filipino Student Bulletin, 6:4, 9, and 19, June, 1927.

Dean, Arthur, "Working Outside School Hours," Journal of Education, 112: 481, July-December, 1930.

Delgado, Francisco A. "In Defense of the Philippines," The Filipino Student Bulletin, 14:1 and 3, November-December 1929.

Dick, McCulloch R., editor. "First Filipino Pilot Gets Commercial license," Philippines Free Press, 29:34, November, 9, 1935.

_____. "New President of U.P.," Philippines Free Press, 28:4, August 18, 1934.

_____. "Thumbnail Sketches of Legislatures," Philippines Free Press, 28:30-38, September 15, 1934.

Fabian, A.C., editor. "Who is Who in the Philippines," Graphic, September 27, 1934. 22-51 pp.

Katigbak, Pedro S., editor. The Filipino Student Bulletin, 7:5, December, 1929.

Mangavil, Florendo R. "Looking Back," The Filipino Student Bulletin, 7:4, April-May, 1934.